SO WHAT ABOUT

HISTORY

?

EDMUND S. MORGAN

SO WHAT ABOUT

HISTORY

ATHENEUM 1969 NEW YORK

"History is bunk,"

said Henry Ford.

He would have been closer if he had said,

"History is junk."

History tells about what we've gotten from the past, and a lot of what we've gotten is junk, things that were useful to our mothers and fathers or their mothers and fathers but no use to us, things that are worn out, things we don't need any more.

Photograph by George Gambsky

Why keep a broken bottle or a bucket with a hole in it or a washing machine that won't run?

7

Photograph by Bob Duncan

For that matter, why keep a house if it is falling apart?

Photograph by George Gambsky

8

Or even a town?

Lake Valley, New Mexico. Photograph by Karl Kernberger

Sometimes people just up and leave a town, as they left this one in New Mexico. People lived here because there was a silver mine nearby. After they took out all the silver, the town was just so much junk to them.

The same thing has happened for thousands of years. Several centuries ago Indians in Arizona decided to junk this cliff town. And about the same time there was a town

Montezuma's Castle, Arizona. Photograph by George Gambsky

in England that nobody wanted any more. The people left it—why we don't know—and gradually its buildings fell down, and dust and dirt covered it up. Now the only way you can see that it was ever there is from an airplane. The streets of the old town are a little lower than the surrounding land. When the sun is low, the shadows show them up, so that a picture taken from the air gives you a kind of map of the old town. The town itself is buried junk.

Newbold Grounds, Catesby, Northamptonshire, England

All junk has a history, and one way of studying history is to study junk. You can find out a good deal about people by studying their junk piles. A thousand years from now, when our cars and washing machines and maybe our houses and towns have become buried junk, somebody may dig them up and try to figure out what sort of people we were.

At Williamsburg, Virginia, people have tried to rebuild the town the way it was 200 years ago, in order that anyone who comes there can see what life was like then. All over the town, wherever it seems likely that there used to be an old house, workers carefully scrape away the dirt with shovels, trowels, and brooms to uncover cellar walls, sidewalks, wells, garden paths, and garden walls, anything that will tell them how the town once looked. They sift the dirt to recover every man-made scrap, every item that may have once been used there. Then they try to fit the broken pieces together like a jigsaw puzzle. Old filled-in wells are an especially good place to dig for things, because they were often used for junk pits.

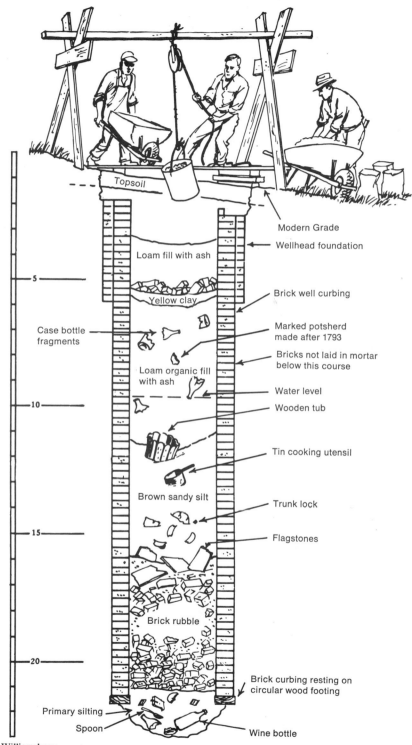

Topsoil

Modern Grade

Wellhead foundation

Loam fill with ash

Brick well curbing

Yellow clay

Case bottle fragments

Marked potsherd made after 1793

Bricks not laid in mortar below this course

Loam organic fill with ash

Water level

Wooden tub

Tin cooking utensil

Brown sandy silt

Trunk lock

Flagstones

Brick rubble

Brick curbing resting on circular wood footing

Primary silting

Spoon

Wine bottle

Colonial Williamsburg

From the junk that comes out of old wells and filled-in cellars, from bits of glass and china, from broken buckles, clay pipes, old spoons, brass buttons, and hundreds of other things we today can begin to guess how people lived in those days. We can tell what they wore, what they drank, what games they played, what jobs they worked at.

Of course there are lots of other clues about the people who lived only two hundred years ago. Their books and newspapers have survived and tell us not only what people bought and sold but also what they thought and did. You can tell quite a lot about life in Williamsburg just from this bunch of advertisements in a 1766 newspaper.

Juſt IMPORTED, *and to be* SOLD *by*
WHOLESALE,
A neat Aſſortment of

European GOODS,

Suitable for the Seaſon.

2‖ GEORGE CRAWFORD.
PETERSBURG, *October* 20, 1766.

Imported from GLASGOW, *ſome time in* May
1765, *by the* PEGGY, *Capt.* ANDREW,

A SMALL BOX, marked M in a diamond, containing CUTLERY, which the ſubſcriber has not received, imagining it has been landed ſomewhere on *James* or *Appamattox* rivers, by miſtake. Whoever gives information of the ſaid box to Mr. *Edward Johnſon*, merchant at *Rocky Ridge*, or to the ſubſcriber, will very much oblige Their moſt humble ſervant,
JAMES MURDOCH.

Halifax county, *Auguſt* 1766.

STRAYED or STOLEN out of my paſture, laſt *Saturday* night, a large gray mare, one of *Crawford's* colts, about 15 hands high, with a hanging mane and ſwitch tail, trots and gallops well, but not branded as I remember. Whoever brings the ſaid mare to me in *Williamſburg* ſhall have TWENTY SHILLINGS reward, and upon conviction of the thief THREE POUNDS.
JAMES SOUTHALL.

OCTOBER 23, 1766.

Taken up, in *Amherſt*, a gray mare, about 4 feet 4 inches high, but not branded; poſted, and appraiſed to 50 s.
‖ ROBERT WRIGHT.

Taken up, in *Mecklenburg*, a gray mare, about 4 feet 3 inches high, about 4 years old, with a whitiſh ſtreak down her face, paces out of hand, her hind feet partly white, dockt, but not branded; poſted, and appraiſed to 3 l. 10 s. ‖ JAMES M'DANIEL, Sen.

Taken up, in *Charlotte*, a bay mare, about 4 feet 8 or 9 inches high, with a few white hairs in her forehead, ſome ſaddle ſpots, paces ſlow, and branded on the near buttock M; poſted, and appraiſed to 9 l.
‖ ROBERT PRICE.

16

JUST IMPORTED,

In the MATTY, *Captain* FOX, *by the subscribers, and to be* SOLD *at their store in* NORFOLK,

A complete assortment of

European GOODS,

Suitable to the Season.

BALFOUR & BARRAUD.

THERE is in GRAY's Creek warehouse a hogshead of TOBACCO, passed by GEORGE KERR, September 18, 1764, No. M, gross 1125, tare 101, neat 1004, which hath never been demanded of the inspectors. 2

To be SOLD, *and* ENTERED *on next* NEW YEAR's *day,*

270 Acres of Land,

WITH houses and orchards, in *Prince George* county, within 2 miles of *Cabin Point*, and very convenient to church and mill. Also 250 acres of strong tobacco and wheat land, with all convenient houses, apple and peach orchards, and the plantation in good order for cropping, lying on *Lizard* creek, in *Brunswick* county, joining the country line, within 3 miles of *Eaton's* ferry, on *Roanoke* river; with crops of corn and fodder, and stock of cattle, hogs, and sheep. Any person inclinable to purchase may know the terms of the first mentioned tract by applying to Mr. *James Fletcher*, living near the premises; and the last mentioned to the subscriber, living on the premises.

JAMES WORTHAM.

To be SOLD *to the highest bidder, on the premises, on* WEDNESDAY *the 12th of* NOVEMBER *next,*

A VERY valuable tract of LAND, in *Lunenburg* county, containing 220 acres, of a good soil for tobacco, with a new dwelling-house, outhouses, and barns, thereon, a fine orchard, and is in good order for cropping, having cleared ground for 8 or 10 hands; being the plantation where Mr. *Benjamin Millner* now lives, and sold by virtue of a deed of trust made us by the said *Millner*. The time of payment will be agreed on at the day of sale.

RICHARD HANSON.
ABRAM SMITH.

GEORGE III. by the grace of God, of *Great Britain*, *France*, and *Ireland*, King, defender of the faith, &c. To the sheriff of *Culpeper* county, greeting: We command you that you summon *Stephen Jett* to appear before our Justices of our General Court, in chancery, at the Capitol in *Williamsburg*, on the first day of the next court, to answer a bill in chancery exhibited against him, and others, by *John Jett*, *John Read*, and *John Shackleford*; and lest he shall in no wise omit, under the penalty of 100 l. and have then there this writ. Witness FRANCIS FAUQUIER, Esq; our Lieutenant Governour, at *Williamsburg*, the 18th day of *October*, in the 6th year of our reign. ‖ BEN. WALLER.

GEORGE III. by the grace of God, of *Great Britain*,

PETERSBURG, *October* 25, 1766.

STRAYED or STOLEN out of my pasture, on *Saturday* night the 11th of this instant, a middle sized black horse, with a star in his forehead, roached mane and short switch tail, paces well when rode, but his brand, if any, forgot.——Whoever brings the said horse to the subscriber shall have FORTY SHILLINGS reward, and if stolen, on conviction of the thief FIVE POUNDS.

‖ ROBERT NEWSUM.

TAKEN up in *November* last, off the mouth of *Rappahannock* river, by *John Gaskins*, deceased, a nine hogshead FLAT, which is appraised to 4 l. 10 s. The owner may have her, on paying as the law directs, by applying to the subscriber, living near the mouth of *Wicomico* river, in *Northumberland* county. 2 ‖ DAVID BALL, Jun.

VIRGINIA, *August* 8, 1766.

COMMITTED to *Frederick* county gaol, on suspicion of being a runaway servant, THOMAS ROBINSON, about 5 feet 6 inches high, about 31 years of age, with black curled hair, and thin look; had on when taken an old hat, osnabrug shirt, and short trousers, says he was born in *Maryland*, in *Prince George's* county, and is a freeman; he has been in *England* the space of 16 years, came from *Liverpool* in the year 1763, and landed at *Silvay's* landing, *Patuxent*, with working his passage over. Whoever has lost such a man is desired to apply to THOMAS CAMPBELL, ‖ Gaoler in *Winchester*.

VIRGINIA, *Sept.* 24, 1766.

COMMITTED to *Frederick* county gaol, on suspicion of being a runaway servant, ROBERT TALBOT, about 5 feet 6 inches high, 63 years of age, of a dark complexion, and says he was born in *London*; had on when committed a brown cut wig, white shirt, tight brown cloth coat, black silk waistcoat, red shag breeches, light blue stockings, and shoes and buckles. Whoever has lost such a man is desired to apply to THOMAS CAMPBELL, ‖ Gaoler in *Winchester*.

Taken up, in *Charlotte*, a dark bay mare, about 4 feet 5 inches high, with a star in her forehead, hanging mane and switch tail, some saddle spots, has a large bell on with a patch marked AA, hinged with a tanned leather collar, and strengthened with a raw leather string, and branded on the near shoulder | ; also a mare colt, foaled last spring; posted, and appraised to 5 l.

‖ JOHN HIGHT.

To be RENTED, *by the* YEAR,

MY plantation, ordinary house, and ferry, at *Sleepy Hole*. The present tenant quits possession *Christmas* next.

I want a single, sober, honest, careful, industrious, active man, an OVERSEER, at my home plantation. I also want a single woman, capable to take the charge of a family as a HOUSEKEEPER. To such persons I will give very good wages. LEMUEL RIDDICK.

NANSEMOND, *October* 25, 1766.

CHESTERFIELD, *October* 13, 1766.

WHEREAS my wife *Margaret Edwards* made her elopement from me the 23d of last month, this is to forewarn all persons from harbouring or crediting her on my account, as I will pay no debts of her contracting after this notice.
2 ‖ MARK EDWARDS.

I HEREBY forewarn all persons

But when we try to study the oldest history, the history, say, of the American Indians before the white man came, or the history of ancient Egypt, sometimes there is very little but old junk to go on, and we treasure every broken bit of pottery because of the help it gives in understanding this part of the past.

But after all, why bother? It may be fun for some people to know about the past, but is it any use? Doesn't it just get in the way of the present? Why not just get rid of the junk and forget it?

One answer is that we can't. We never really do get rid of all the things we get from the past. Some things today are just as they were centuries ago. Some things, of course, we change in one way or another.

We turn some junk into new, useful things. Even old auto bodies can be used to make something else. We build huge machines for smashing them into blocks that can be melted down and made into new autos or washing machines or refrigerators.

Courtesy of Harris Press and Shear Corporation

In the same way people have always turned old and useless things into new and useful ones. Twenty-five hundred years ago the people of Athens had to build a wall in a hurry in order to protect their city against its enemies. The Athenians wrecked old buildings and even raided graveyards for the materials to build their wall with. You can still see parts of it today, a pretty messy wall, made of different kinds of stone and broken chunks of pillars. But it served its purpose.

People have often built new houses out of old ones. Sometimes instead of wrecking old buildings they have simply put them to new uses. Two thousand years ago, when the

Romans controlled most of Europe, they built huge outdoor arenas in their great cities, where the public could watch fights between gladiators or see condemned prisoners eaten by wild animals. After these bloody shows were stopped, people often tore down the arenas in order to use the stones for other buildings or for paving roads. But in some places they simply turned the arenas into apartment houses. At Arles in southern France, a thousand years after the Romans left, two hundred families were living inside the walls of the arena.

from Joseph Seguin, *Les Antiquitez d'Arles* (Arles, 1687)

The partition walls and roofs in the arena were later taken down and the building put back to something like its original purpose. Today it is used for bullfights.

French Cultural Services

But other things from the past we keep right on using in the same way that their first makers used them. You probably pass every day houses that are older than anyone who lives in them.

BUILT
ABOUT 1740

Photograph by the author Newport, Rhode Island

If you lived in Europe you might have a house built several hundred years ago, and you might even ride to school over a bridge built by the Romans, like this one.

French Cultural Services

The bridge is in front with the car going over it. The higher wall behind it is part of an aqueduct, which the Romans built for bringing water (it flowed along the top) to the nearby city. The aqueduct is no longer used, but it is still good to look at.

We keep some things from the past just because they are good to look at. Sometimes in the buried junk of the past people find things that give as much pleasure to us as to the original owners, like this statue of a boy on a horse that lay buried in the sea for two thousand years. It was pulled out a few years ago (but the horse got away!).

Royal Greek Embassy

Modern sculptors have recently discovered that beautiful things can be found in our own junk yards. Here is a collection of junk that is now on exhibition in an art museum.

Richard Stankiewicz.
Kabuki Dancer. 1956.
Steel and cast iron.
80¼" high.
Collection Whitney Museum
of American Art,
New York.

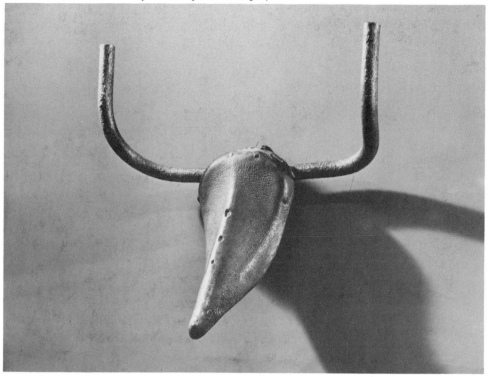

Pablo Picasso took an old bicycle seat and a pair of handle bars and turned them into the head of a bull.

Some things we keep just because they remind us of good times. Do you have any souvenirs? Sometimes we try to protect old things because they make us feel at home. They have become part of us, and we don't like to see them go, even if we need a new freeway right where they happen to be.

Drawing by Robert Day, © 1967 by
The *New Yorker* Magazine, Inc.

Long-lived Ideas

SO A LOT OF THINGS we get from the past seem worth keeping for one reason or another. But we get more than just things from the past. We also get ideas and ways of doing things. That is how we differ from most other animals. A bird does not learn from its parents how to build a nest. Somehow or other it knows without being shown. But could you build a clock or a washing machine without being shown? We know how to build houses and bridges and clocks and a thousand other things because we have been taught by people who built them before.

Columbus showed the people of Spain how to cross the Atlantic Ocean and get back again. After he had found the way, lots of people began crossing the ocean in search of new homes. But if everyone who wanted to cross the ocean had had to figure out for himself how to do it, not many would have made it, and we would probably not be living in America now.

We have people today like Columbus who keep figuring out how to do new things like making rockets that will reach the moon. But there would be no time for new things if we had to figure out by ourselves how to make the old familiar ones we need. An easy way to cut a piece of wood in two is by using a saw, but it is a good thing you don't have to invent the saw every time you want to cut something. Wheels seem like a pretty obvious way of getting something from one place to another, but the people Columbus found in America had never thought of a wheel, and nobody had shown them how to make one. So they and their dogs had to drag loads along the ground on poles.

Ideas are passed on by talking and writing, two of the world's greatest inventions. By talking, someone who knows how to do a thing can tell everybody else how, and by writing he can tell people he never saw and never will see, people who have not even been born yet. To make this possible, we sometimes have to invent new words—you probably have taught your parents a few. But most of the words that you and other Americans use every day are the same as the ones spoken by the first Englishmen who landed in America more than 350 years ago.

Those words were invented over a long period of time by Englishmen, but the inventors made most of their new words out of older Latin or French or Anglo-Saxon words, much as they might have used stone from an old Roman arena to build a new house or pave a road. The letters with which we spell or write words also go back to the Romans, who in turn borrowed many of them from the Greeks.

You can see how closely we still imitate the Romans by looking carefully at the shape of the capital letters in this or almost any other book. A magnifying glass will show that the lines of which a letter is made (especially capital letters) are thicker in some places and thinner in others and that the ends of the lines sometimes have small points attached to them. The letters have this shape partly because of the problems that Greek and Roman stonecutters had in cutting letters. To cut letters on stone, the workman tapped a chisel

along both sides of a line to make a V-shaped groove. When the groove was long enough, it was hard to finish if off neatly. The best way was to chisel a special cut, called a "serif", across the ends and to widen the main groove a little as it got close to the serif.

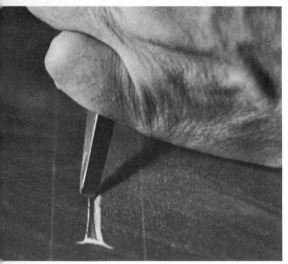

If you look at the capital "I"s on this page, you will see that they still have the shape they got from the Roman stonecutter's chisel, narrow in the middle, widening at the top and bottom, and finished off with a serif at each end. Most other capital letters have serifs too, wherever a straight line in them comes to an end without meeting another line.

From *The Elements of Lettering* by Benson and Carey. Copyright 1950 by McGraw-Hill, Inc. Used with permission of McGraw-Hill Book Company.

Photographs by the author at the John Stevens Shop, Newport, R.I.

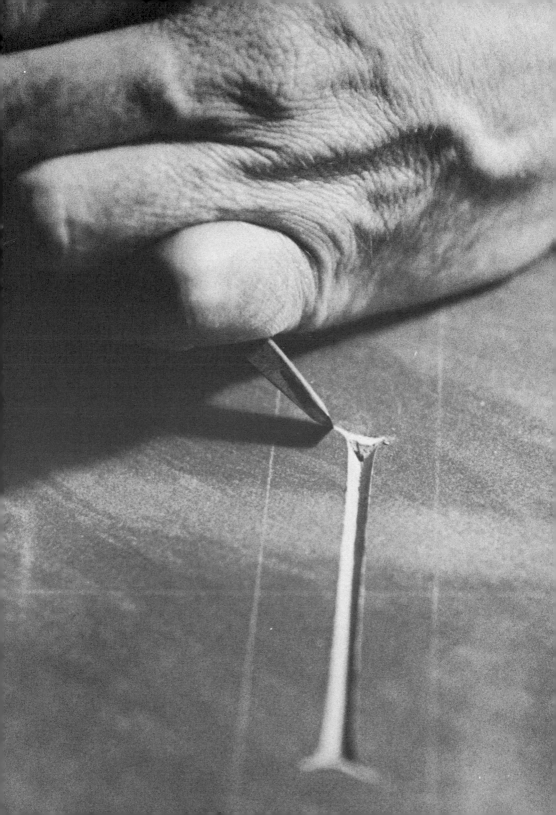

Some people think it is foolish to be so tied down to the past in this way. They have designed letters without serifs and without the differences in thickness that originated in stone cutting. They call their new printing "sanserif" (meaning without serifs), and you sometimes see it in the headlines of newspapers and on billboards. This paragraph is printed in sanserif letters. But the old Roman type of letters is still the one that printers use most often, perhaps because most people find it more pleasing to the eye or perhaps just because they are used to it.

If in America, the New World, we speak with words invented before our continent was discovered and print with letters in a shape invented by the Romans, it is not surprising that there are other ways in which our New World has kept on using old ideas. For example, in the Dutch colony of Surinam in South America, Africans brought in as slaves carried with them memories of intricate open-work designs used to decorate important things, like this chair belonging to the traditional ruler of Agogo in Ghana. The chair was made before 1800, perhaps as early as 1700.

Asipim Agogohene. Photograph by Peter Moore.
Reproduced by courtesy of Robert Harris Thompson
and the Museum of Primitive Art, from *African
and Afro-American Art : The Transatlantic Tradition.*

Today the free descendants of those slaves still decorate
things like this window grill with similar designs.

Collected in Surinam in 1955.
American Museum of Natural History.
Courtesy of Robert Harris Thompson.

In the same way settlers all over the New World built houses like the ones they remembered from the Old World. The first Englishmen who settled in the American wilderness did not live in log cabins, as many people think they did, because it did not occur to them to build a house that way. They had no idea of a log cabin. They came from English towns, where houses were made of brick or stone or of wood that had been smoothly cut into boards by a sawmill. In America they built their houses the same way, even though they had no sawmills in the wilderness and had to

cut trees into boards by hand. Later, settlers from the forests of Sweden, where people did live in log cabins, first built these simpler houses in America and taught the other settlers to do it. This is one of the first pictures ever made of an American log cabin.

from Basil Hall, *Forty Etchings* (Edinburgh, 1829)

As the English colonies in America grew older and more prosperous, the colonists built bigger and fancier houses. And, like the earlier settlers, they continued to make their houses look like English ones. It probably never occurred to them to build any other way.

Cottage at Brenchley, Kent, England

Photograph by Samuel Chamberlain

Richard Jackson House, Portsmouth, New Hampshire

from Thomas Harwood, *The History and Antiquities of the Church and City of Lichfield* (Gloucester, 1806)

Ediall Hall, Staffordshire, England

Governor's Palace, Williamsburg, Virginia

Even when we do give up an old idea, we don't always re-place it with a brand new one. Instead, we are likely to turn to some other old idea, perhaps even older than the one we give up. When the American colonists broke their connec-tions with England and began the United States, they gave up some ideas they had brought from England, but they reached farther back into the past for other ideas to help them. From the junk pile of history they picked an idea that had been dumped there thousands of years earlier. They were trying to build a government for their new nation, for they believed (as we still do) that all men need government to protect them from thieves and bullies in their midst and to defend them from foreign enemies. They might have made a government just like the English one, because they thought the English government was the best in Europe. But

Roman Forum

Illinois Information Service

England had a king and queen and hundreds of dukes and earls and other noblemen, and Americans knew from history that kings and queens and noblemen had often caused trouble.

History also told them about the republics of ancient Greece and Rome, which had been run entirely by the people, without any kings or noblemen to help or hinder them. They decided to make the United States a republic, without kings or noblemen. And in order to be sure it stayed that way, they got together in 1787 and wrote a Constitution, a set of laws that said how the people were to choose their own government and what that government could do and what it could not do. The laws worked. The United States is still a republic, and the Constitution made in 1787 (with a few changes made since then) is still its "supreme law."

Just as Americans are still using an old idea about government that they adopted almost two hundred years ago, most of us use old ideas all the time. We accept them and seldom think about them. We all come into the world as members of a family, in which we learn to walk, talk, speak, think, and act like the other members. Our mothers and fathers learned in the same way from *their* mothers and fathers. By the time we leave our family group to start a new family of our own, we have likes and dislikes and skills and habits we can never forget. And we pass these lessons from the past on to our own children.

Carol Perkins

Susanne Szasz

Like the family, other groups or "institutions" keep alive ideas from the past. For groups, like ideas and buildings, can last longer than the people who start them. A business company, for example, may outlast its founders.

A club may be older than any of its members. Most towns are older than the oldest inhabitant.

Many religious groups, or churches, began centuries ago.

1707

THE FIRST
CONGREGATIONAL
CHURCH

· MINISTERS ·
Rev. Franklin A. Bower
Rev. Charles Wm. Gelbach

Photographs by the author

Every group we belong to expects us to accept its ideas, customs, or rules, and usually the most important of these are the oldest ones, the ones the group began with. Usually we do what the group expects and hardly notice that we are doing it. For instance, we all belong to towns or cities, counties, states, and the United States. Each of these groups has books full of laws that we are expected to obey. And many of the laws were made before we were born. The United States Constitution began, as we saw, in 1787 and was itself based on much older ideas.

If we do not often notice the many laws of our city, state, and country, it is because we have grown up as members of these groups and automatically do what the group requires. It does not occur to most drivers, for example, to drive on

the left-hand side of the street. If anyone took a fancy to do so and did not die at once in a head-on collision, he would quickly feel the force of the group. He would be arrested, fined, and if he kept on driving that way, he might be put in prison or be deprived of the right to drive, because every state in the United States decided long ago that everyone must drive on the right. In England, on the other hand, the state decided long ago that everyone must drive on the left, and Englishmen must therefore obey that rule.

Groups are the great keepers of ideas from the past. Families and governments, churches and clubs may stick to rules or to ways of doing things for hundreds of years. They stick to them until for some reason people get tired of the ideas or are no longer able to make them work. But if people do discard an idea, that is not necessarily the end of it. Ideas, unlike the men who think them up, need not die. Ideas may go on being used indefinitely, as long as people need or like them. But they may also lie unused for centuries and then spring to life again, like the republic. As long as a trace of an idea remains, on paper, parchment, clay, or stone, it may reach someone who likes it and be used again. Ideas are hard to kill.

Changing Times

THE PAST COMES INTO OUR LIVES at every moment. It is there in what we see, what we think, and what we do. And yet we know that the present is not the same as the past. We do not think and do exactly as our parents and teachers think and do or as they thought and did when they were our age. Indeed we often seem to think quite the opposite from them. Do you and your parents agree, for example, on how a person should wear his hair? For better or worse, every minute, every year, every century is different from the last one. But what is different? Why did a difference happen? And how? These are questions that historians ask and try, not always successfully, to answer.

Of course, sometimes the answer is easy. Consider a simple kind of change that is always taking place. We have noticed that the past is a great storehouse of ideas and that ideas may have a long life. They can, nevertheless, be killed,

and some of them deserve to be. A thousand years ago people had some pretty strange ideas about animals. They believed in animals that did not exist at all, like the griffin and
the manticore.

from T. H. White, *A Book of Beasts*

They believed that in some parts of the world there were
men with one leg, with heads below their shoulders, with
horns and other oddities.

52

Hartmann Schedel, *Liber Chronicarum* (Nürnberg, 1943), Yale University Library

They even had mistaken ideas about real animals that lived around them. They thought, for example, that the fish hawk had one webbed foot (like a duck) and one clawed foot (like an eagle), so that it would have looked like this.

Now you only had to take a close look at a fish hawk to see that both its feet were clawed and not webbed. And some-

Photo by Howard H. Cleaves

times fishermen or hunters must have had the chance to notice what the bird was really like. Nevertheless the mistaken idea lived on for hundreds of years. It did not die until the sixteenth century, when men began to test ideas by looking at the world around them more closely and more carefully than people had ever looked before. They looked at the fish hawk and they saw two clawed feet.

Ulyssis Aldrovandus,
Ornithologiae hoc est de Avibus Historiae Libri XII
(Bonon, 1599), Yale University Library

The old idea of the fish hawk and many other old ideas died because people at last saw that they were wrong. But it is not always easy to look and see that an idea is wrong. Before Columbus discovered America and Magellan sailed around the world, people in Europe could believe that all sorts of fantastic creatures lived in distant places for they could not get to these distant places to see that there were no one-legged men or men without heads. The Greeks believed that the sun traveled around and around the earth, and they seemed to be right. Everyone could look and see the sun coming up in the morning on one side of the earth and going down at night on the other side. It was not until someone invented a telescope so that men could look and really see how the solar system worked that the idea could be proved wrong.

The same was true of ideas about the atom. We have known for a long time that everything in the world is made up of atoms and that atoms are so small they cannot be seen even with our most powerful microscopes. But even though we cannot see atoms, scientists have recently invented instruments like the linear accelerator to test the way atoms act, and from the way they act scientists can tell that many

Brookhaven National Laboratory

of our ideas about them have been wrong. It used to be thought, for example, that atoms were the smallest thing in existence and could not be divided into still smaller parts. Now we have found out that atoms contain several different parts, which leave interesting paths of bubbles behind them as they pass through a "bubble chamber", and scientists are busy finding out how these mysterious parts fit together.

58

Brookhaven National Laboratory

People have been looking, seeing, and giving up wrong ideas ever since the first man had the first idea. But an idea doesn't have to be proved wrong to lose out. Sometimes we give up an old idea simply because someone thinks up another idea that we like better. After the American colonists declared their independence from England in 1776, some people wanted to have new American buildings for the new American republic. Thomas Jefferson traveling in France saw the ruins of an ancient Roman temple that he thought

from C. L. Clérisseau, *Antiquités de la France,*
J. G. Legrand, ed., Paris, 1804. Yale University Library.

Maison Carrée

was the most beautiful building he had ever seen. He sent
home a model of it to serve as a pattern for the state capitol
of Virginia.

Virginia State Library

Virginia State Library

There was nothing wrong with the English-style buildings formerly built in America; but people were ready for a change, and it seemed appropriate for the new republic to copy the buildings of the old republics of Greece and Rome. The idea spread. Books were printed with drawings of Greek and Roman temples for builders to copy. And temples or temple-like buildings sprang up all over the United States for use as government offices, banks, business firms, churches, and private houses.

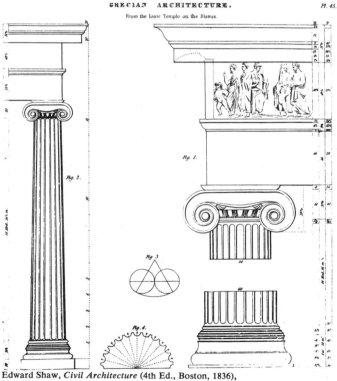

GRECIAN ARCHITECTURE.

From the Ionic Temple on the Ilissus.

Pl. 45.

Edward Shaw, *Civil Architecture* (4th Ed., Boston, 1836), Yale University Library.

But within fifty years people were tired of temples. It was silly, they decided, to try to make everything in the same shape no matter what it was used for. In their opinion, the outside of a building ought to fit whatever was needed inside the building. American buildings needed fireplaces for heat, and fireplaces needed chimneys. But a Greek temple looked pretty funny if it had a lot of chimneys sticking out of its roof. A temple was supposed to have its windows and doors in particular places. But an American bank or house might need its windows or doors in other places. And so Americans stopped copying the Greeks.

63

They turned instead to a style that had been popular in Europe hundreds of years later, at a time that is now called the Middle Ages. The "Gothic" style buildings of the Middle Ages had a great variety of shapes. You could put doors, windows, fireplaces, stairs, and rooms wherever you wanted them. No matter how irregular the outside of the building turned out to be, it still seemed to look all right. The Gothic houses, banks, and churches that Americans put up everywhere had many different shapes. Some were so varied that they looked like giant frosted wedding cakes.

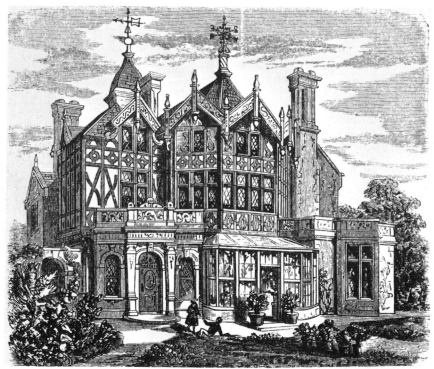

from C. J. Richardson *House Building from a Cottage to a Mansion* (New York, 1873)

Photograph by Wayne Andrews

Change comes every time people give up one idea and put another one in its place, even if the new idea is really an old one. When an old idea is revived, it is never quite the same in its modern setting as it was originally. The republican government of the United States is not just the same as the republican governments of ancient Greece. The Gothic buildings of the nineteenth century were not quite the same as those of the thirteenth century.

And sometimes changes are entirely new and not simply a matter of getting rid of one old idea in favor of another old idea. Precisely because men are able to use old ideas, because they can start where their fathers left off and not have to invent saws and wheels and automobiles, they can give some time to inventing really new things and thinking new thoughts. In the twentieth century architects have thought of really new shapes for buildings, unlike any in the past, and they have been helped in doing so by engineers and scientists who have invented new materials and new and stronger ways of putting old materials together.

There are many other kinds of change that make one year or century different from another. But the changes that historians study most are changes in the way that people live together, changes in the groups they belong to and in the rules or laws that groups make their members obey. Even though groups preserve the past, they do keep changing. They grow, and they shrink. Old groups disappear, and new ones start up. They change their rules, and they change their rulers. And all this is as true of the most powerful groups, which we call nations, as it is of others.

66

Some changes happen without anybody planning them or thinking much about them in advance. A hundred years ago three-quarters of the American people lived in the country or in small towns. Today almost three-quarters of the American people live in cities.

Nobody decided that Americans ought to live in cities. There was nothing wrong with the idea of living in the country, the way there was with the old idea of the fish hawk. The towns just grew into cities as people moved there to get jobs and to be closer to other people.

Most important changes in living together have happened less easily than the change from town life to city life. They have happened because people wanted very much to make them and worked very hard to make them. When people begin to think that something in their way of living together is

Alexander Alland

bad, evil, cruel, or unfair, they want to stop it. But usually
not everyone in the group agrees about how bad it is or
whether it is bad at all. Then people may argue for years before the group can be persuaded to change its ways. Nowa-
days we think that the bloody shows that took place in the

Roman arenas were a horrible evil, but they kept going for centuries before people at last saw that they were evil and stopped them.

When the United States government began, the Constitution did not give women the right to vote. In the 1830's women began to ask why not. It was unfair, they said, for men to have the whole say in government. This may seem pretty obvious today, but for a long time men opposed it with arguments like this:

DANGER!

Woman's Suffrage Would Double the Irresponsible Vote

It is a MENACE to the Home, Men's Employment and to All Business

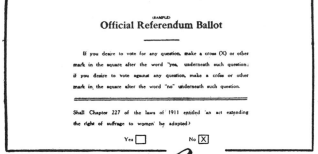

(SAMPLE)
Official Referendum Ballot

If you desire to vote for any question, make a cross (X) or other mark in the square after the word "yes, underneath such question; if you desire to vote against any question, make a cross or other mark in the square after the word "no" underneath such question.

Shall Chapter 227 of the laws of 1911 entitled 'an act extending the right of suffrage to women' be adopted?

Yes ☐   No ☒

The above is an exact reproduction of the separate ballot printed on **pink** paper which will be handed to you in your voting place on November 5. Be sure and put your cross (X) in the square after the word "no" as shown here, and—**be sure and vote this pink ballot.**

Issued and Circulated by
PROGRESS PUBLISHING CO
WATERTOWN, WIS.

But women kept arguing and working for a change in the
Constitution that would give them the vote. And finally in
1917 they succeeded. A group of people who want a change
can usually get it if they work hard enough and long enough
at it.

State Historical Society of Wisconsin

Often the people who are against a change feel as strongly as those who are for it, and neither side is able to persuade the other. Eventually the argument may turn into a fight. The United States had such a fight about slavery. A hundred and fifty years ago more than a million Americans were slaves, owned by other Americans. The slaves had to work for their owners (who gave them clothes and food and a place to live), and everything they earned by their work belonged to their owners. If a slave married and had children, they too belonged to his owner. When Americans first began to see the evil of slavery and tried to get rid of it, many of the people who owned slaves thought it was bad and set their slaves free. But most slave owners refused to do so, because they did not want to lose the money they had paid to buy their slaves and because they did not think that slavery was as bad as other people supposed.

As slavery continued in the southern states, more and more people in the North (where there were no slaves) argued that the government ought not to allow so evil a thing to exist in the United States. Hundreds of books and papers were printed to persuade people to stop it.

GOD AGAINST SLAVERY:

AND THE

FREEDOM AND DUTY OF THE PULPIT

TO REBUKE IT,

AS A SIN AGAINST GOD.

THE

TESTIMONY OF GOD

AGAINST SLAVERY:

A

COLLECTION OF PASSAGES FROM THE BIBLE.

WHICH SHOW THE

SIN OF HOLDING AND TREATING THE HUMAN
SPECIES AS PROPERTY.

WITH NOTES.

TO WHICH IS ADDED

THE TESTIMONY OF THE CIVILIZED V

AGAINST SLAVE

BY REV. LA ROY SUNⁱ

DESPOTISM IN AMERICA:

AN INQUIRY

INTO

THE NATURE, RESULTS, AND LEGAL BASIS

OF THE

SLAVE-HOLDING SYSTEM

UNITED STATES.

AMERICAN SLAVERY

AS IT IS:

AN

APPEAL

IN FAVOR OF THAT CLASS

OF

TESTIMONY

AMERICANS CALLED AFRICANS.

OF

A THOUSAND WITNESSES.

The more the southerners heard of the arguments, the more they objected to being told what to do by the North. They worried that the northerners might try to take away their slaves and set them free. Finally the southerners tried to cut their connections with the United States and become a separate country, so that the North could not interfere with them. But the northern states were not willing to end the argument that way. They made war to force the southerners to stay part of the United States. After four years of fighting, the North won. And since many northerners were just as eager to end the evil of slavery as they were to keep the United States together, the end of the war meant the end of slavery. Slavery ended because the majority of Americans wanted it to end. The change came because people argued, worked, and finally fought for it.

History, then, is not just about things that have stayed the same or have been used over and over again. It is also the story of change: change in ideas, change in ways of building, dressing, and doing things, change in the way we live together, peaceful change and violent change, changes we like and changes we don't like. It has to do with the choices people make between old ideas and new, between old ways of doing things and new untried ways. We have seen that changes are not always easy to bring about, that a great deal of the past has lived on into the present. But changes do come, and it is interesting to ask ourselves just how much change we ourselves can make or want to make in the world we have inherited from the past.

74

These are not easy questions, and few of us know ourselves or the world we live in well enough to be sure of the answers. But by looking at some of the biggest changes in the American past, perhaps we can learn a little about ourselves and about how much change people have been able to make when they set their minds to it.

How Much Change

THERE IS A WORD for the biggest changes in the world. We call them "revolutions." The word can be used in many ways. We speak of the "Copernican Revolution," when we mean the change in thinking brought about by Copernicus' idea that the earth goes around the sun instead of the sun going around the earth. The Industrial Revolution was the change from making things by hand to making them by machine. But usually we use the word "revolution" for the change that comes when a group of people overthrow their government by force and change the laws by which they are governed. This kind of change is likely to affect more people and to affect them more than any other kind of change. The Russians had a revolution in 1917 when they overthrew and killed their Czar and started a communist government. The French had a revolution in 1789 when they overthrew and killed their king and started a republican government. And

the Americans had a revolution in 1776 when they overthrew the government that England had placed over them.

After a successful revolution the winners often want to
change their whole society. They feel that everything must
be made somehow different and better. With the old government gone, it seems like an opportunity to wipe the black-
board clean and make a fresh start. They think it is a time to
put the whole past on the junk heap, a time to become a new
and different and better people.

How much of the past can men give up when they have a
revolution? The answer is, of course, different for every revolution. But if we look at the American Revolution, we will
see that it did not get rid of as much as some of the Revolu-
tionists wanted to get rid of.

When the Revolution began, some Americans wanted to
rub out the old boundaries between the colonies. The King
of England had set those boundaries when the colonies were
founded. He had separated Virginia from North Carolina,
Massachusetts from Connecticut, and so on. Americans
from thirteen colonies, all next to each other, had now
joined to fight the King. They were a single people, a new
nation that should not be split up by old boundaries. "I am
not a Virginian," cried Patrick Henry, "but an American."
Virginia was something created by the King of England. It
must be no more.

Thomas Jefferson thought that Americans, having made
a break from their English past, should from now on keep a
permanent break between past and present. "The earth be-

longs to the living," he declared, and he wanted American governments always to pay the bills right away for all their expenses, so that new generations would not have to pay for things that a past generation had done.

Noah Webster, a Connecticut schoolmaster, favored still another kind of change. He thought that the Americans should give up the old spelling they had inherited from England and should instead spell words the way they sound. For example, "enough" would be spelled "enuf." "Laugh" would be "laf." "Head" would be "hed."

P R E F A C E. xi

IN the eſſays, ritten within the laſt yeer, a conſiderable change of ſpelling iz introduced by way of experiment. This liberty waz taken by the writers before the age of queen Elizabeth, and to this we are indeted for the preference of modern ſpelling over that of Gower and Chaucer. The man who admits that the change of *houſbonde, mynde, ygone, moneth* into *huſband, mind, gone, month,* iz an improovment, muſt acknowlege alſo the riting of *hellh, breth, rong, tung, munth,* to be an improovment. There iz no alternativ. Every poſſible reezon that could ever be offered for altering the ſpelling of wurds, ſtil exiſts in full force ; and if a gradual reform ſhould not be made in our language, it wil proov that we are leſs under the influence of reezon than our anceſtors.

Hartford, June, 1790.

from *A Collection of Essays and Fugitiv Writings* (Boston, 1790)

Not many Americans were willing to get rid of as much of the past as Jefferson or Henry or Webster. They were not willing to free the living from the debts of the past, as Jefferson recommended. In fact, they passed on many of the bills for the Revolutionary War itself to their children. Nor did Virginia disappear. The boundaries of the thirteen colonies did not melt away. With only a few changes they still exist as the boundaries of the thirteen states, and those states still have the same names they had when they were colonies.

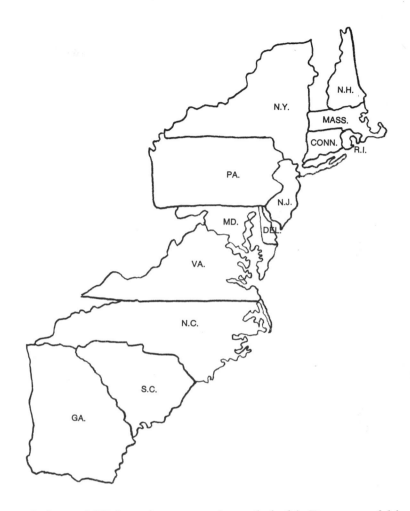

A few of Webster's proposals took hold. Because of his influence words ending in "our" in England now end in "or" in the United States. We write "color" instead of "colour" and "labor" instead of "labour." But for the most part Americans went right on with the spelling they had learned from England, and even Webster himself gave up his idea. He started the dictionary we now use.

In fact, the Americans kept so much of what they had before that people have been arguing ever since as to just what the Revolution was all about. Some have even called it a "conservative" revolution, saying that the Americans were not trying to change anything, that all they wanted was to keep things that England was trying to change. One thing is sure. Before 1776 Americans had a king. After 1776 they did not. And they did not want one. Kings, they decided, were historical junk.

Pulling down the statue of George III in New York, 1776

But the junking of the king was not as great a change as you might think. Although Americans wanted no more kings or noblemen, they did like many things about the English government. These things they copied into their own new republican governments. They even kept some things that at first seemed to be useless to a country without a king. A good example was the Bill of Rights, which was England's way of controlling kings.

At the time of the American Revolution England had had a king for as long as anyone could remember. And for just as long, Englishmen had struggled to get their kings to agree that the people had certain rights that the king must respect. In the year 1215 a group of barons, powerful men who headed the king's army, had forced King John to agree to the *Magna Carta,* which was a whole list of rights. The barons had claimed these rights mainly for themselves, but in later years other Englishmen demanded the same rights and got them.

The rights that the English made their kings agree to were mostly for the purpose of preventing him from injuring them. For example, the right to "trial by jury" meant that the king could not put a man in prison unless it was proved in court that the man had broken a law. In court the king's lawyers had to persuade a jury, that is a group of twelve of the man's neighbors, men like himself. He could not be imprisoned unless all twelve agreed that he was really guilty. The man also had the right to be helped by a lawyer, someone who knew all about the laws and could therefore prevent the king's lawyers from tricking him. And so on.

Englishmen thought these rights were very important, and so did the colonists. But when the colonies got rid of the king in 1776 (because they thought he had violated some of their rights) was there any more need for a bill of rights? A bridle is good for controlling a horse, but do you need one if you don't have a horse? The men who wrote the Constitution of the United States in 1787 decided that Americans had no need for a bill of rights because they had no king.

But many people disagreed. They felt uneasy about a government without a bill of rights. Maybe some of them were not quite sure why. But on thinking it over, the majority of Americans decided that they did want a bill of rights. Even though they had no king to guard against and even though their new government was to be run by the people and for the people, they were afraid that there might come times when the people needed protection against themselves. If some of the people tried to violate the rights of the rest, then a bill of rights might be just as useful to protect people from people as it had been to protect people from kings. So one of the first things Americans did after agreeing to the United States Constitution was to add a bill of rights to it. In the Bill of Rights they stated that the people who governed them could not do the things that the King of England could not do and a few other things besides.

Congress of the United States,

begun and held at the City of New-York, on

Wednesday, the fourth of March, one thousand seven hundred and eighty nine.

THE Conventions of a number of the States having, at the time of their adopting the Constitution, expressed a desire, in order to prevent misconstruction or abuse of its powers, that further declaratory and restrictive clauses should be added: And as extending the ground of public confidence in the Government, will best ensure the beneficent ends of its institution.

RESOLVED, by the Senate and House of Representatives of the United States of America in Congress assembled, two thirds of both Houses concurring, that the following Articles be proposed to the Legislatures of the several States, as amendments to the Constitution of the United States, all, or any of which articles, when ratified by three fourths of the said Legislatures, to be valid to all intents and purposes, as part of the said Constitution; viz.

ARTICLES in addition to, and Amendment of the Constitution of the United States of America, proposed by Congress, and ratified by the Legislatures of the several States, pursuant to the fifth Article of the original Constitution.

Article the first ... After the first enumeration required by the first article of the Constitution, there shall be one Representative for every thirty thousand, until the number shall amount to one hundred, after which the proportion shall be so regulated by Congress, that there shall be not less than one hundred Representatives, nor less than one Representative for every forty thousand persons, until the number of Representatives shall amount to two hundred, after which the proportion shall be so regulated by Congress, that there shall not be less than two hundred Representatives, nor more than one Representative for every fifty thousand persons.

Article the second ... No law, varying the compensation for the services of the Senators and Representatives, shall take effect, until an election of Representatives shall have intervened.

Article the third ... Congress shall make no law respecting an establishment of religion, or prohibiting the free exercise thereof; or abridging the freedom of speech, or of the press; or the right of the people peaceably to assemble, and to petition the Government for a redress of grievances.

Article the fourth ... A well regulated Militia, being necessary to the security of a free State, the right of the people to keep and bear Arms, shall not be infringed.

Article the fifth ... No Soldier shall, in time of peace be quartered in any house, without the consent of the owner, nor in time of war, but in a manner to be prescribed by law.

Article the sixth ... The right of the people to be secure in their persons, houses, papers, and effects, against unreasonable searches and seizures, shall not be violated, and no Warrants shall issue, but upon probable cause, supported by oath or affirmation, and particularly describing the place to be searched, and the persons or things to be seized.

Article the seventh ... No person shall be held to answer for a capital, or otherwise infamous crime, unless on a presentment or indictment of a grand jury, except in cases arising in the land or naval forces, or in the Militia, when in actual service in time of War or public danger; nor shall any person be subject for the same offence to be twice put in jeopardy of life or limb; nor shall be compelled in any criminal case, to be a witness against himself, nor be deprived of life, liberty, or property, without due process of law; nor shall private property be taken for public use without just compensation.

Article the eighth ... In all criminal prosecutions, the accused shall enjoy the right to a speedy and public trial, by an impartial jury of the State and district wherein the crime shall have been committed, which district shall have been previously ascertained by law, and to be informed of the nature and cause of the accusation; to be confronted with the witnesses against him; to have compulsory process for obtaining witnesses in his favor, and to have the assistance of counsel for his defence.

Article the ninth ... In suits at common law, where the value in controversy shall exceed twenty dollars, the right of trial by jury shall be preserved, and no fact tried by a jury shall be otherwise re-examined in any Court of the United States, than according to the rules of the common law.

Article the tenth ... Excessive bail shall not be required, nor excessive fines imposed, nor cruel and unusual punishments inflicted.

Article the eleventh ... The enumeration in the Constitution, of certain rights, shall not be construed to deny or disparage others retained by the people.

Article the twelfth ... The powers not delegated to the United States by the Constitution, nor prohibited by it to the States, are reserved to the States respectively, or to the people.

Frederick Augustus Muhlenberg Speaker of the House of Representatives.

ATTEST,

John Adams, Vice-President of the United States, and President of the Senate.

John Beckley, Clerk of the House of Representatives.

Sam. A. Otis Secretary of the Senate.

The Bill of Rights

Some people doubted that the Bill of Rights would work. After all, the American government was run entirely by the people. If most of the people really wanted to do something, they could pass a law to do it. They could even abolish the Bill of Rights and take away the right of trial by jury and every other right. But the doubters seem so far to have been wrong. So far no rights have been removed from the Constitution, and some have been added to it. Once in a while someone attacks the Bill of Rights, saying, for example, that its protection of free speech gives too much help to people who criticize the government, or that it helps criminals get away, because it stops policemen from going into a private house without a court order. But most Americans believe that the Bill of Rights is still a useful and necessary protection for everyone. When it is attacked, they defend it. And it defends them, in the same way as the old *Magna Carta* defended Englishmen against their king.

In the year 1962 the United States Supreme Court received a letter written from prison by a man named Clarence Earl Gideon. He said that he had been put there by a court in Florida for a robbery he did not do. Of course many people who have done wrong claim that they did not. But Gideon said that at his trial he had not been allowed to have the help of a lawyer. The Supreme Court read the records of the Florida court and found that what Gideon said was true. He really had not been given a lawyer to help him. That was against the Bill of Rights. It is the job of the United States Supreme Court to prevent the government from doing anything against the Constitution, including anything against the Bill of Rights. So the Supreme Court ordered the prison to set Gideon free. Then the court in Florida gave him a new trial for the same crime, this time with a lawyer helping him, and the lawyer was able to prove that Gideon was not guilty. The Bill of Rights saved him.

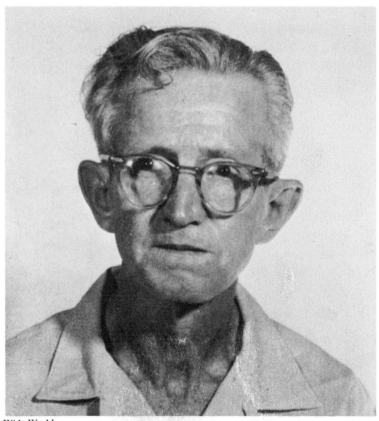

Wide World

I was sentenced to The State Penitentiary by The Circuit Court of Bay County, State of Florida. The present proceeding was commenced on a petition for a Writ of Habeus Corpus To The Supreme Court of The State of Florida To vacate The sentence, on the grounds that I was made to stand Trial without The aid of counsel, and, at all times of my incarseretion. The said Court refused To appoint counsel and therefore deprived me of Due process of law, and violate my rights in The Bill of Rights and the constitution of the United States.

Clarence Earl Gideon

5th day of Jan 1962 Petitioner

Lawrence C Duzza

NOTARY PUBLIC

Notary Public, State ... at Large
My Commission ... Sept. 19, 1962
Bonded by American Surety Co. of N.Y.

Gideon's Letter to the Supreme Court
John F. Davis, Clerk, Supreme Court of the United States

Perhaps the reason we stick to these old ways of government is that cases like Gideon's keep coming up. Governments are supposed to protect people. That is why we have them. But in the twentieth century, as in every previous one, governments keep going wrong. They often hurt the people they are supposed to help, like Hitler's government in Germany in the 1930's and 1940's, or Mussolini's in Italy, or Stalin's in Russia. Over the years we have learned only very slowly about government. But one thing we have found out, that certain rules, including those in the Bill of Rights, help to keep our own government doing what it is supposed to do. When those rules seem to be causing trouble, we are inclined to be stubborn about changing them. We may not always be sure why, but we suspect that they are more useful than they seem at the moment.

When we look at other people's revolutions, we see that most of them, like ours, have kept much from the past. If history gives us junk, then, it also gives us some solid and durable furniture, old and reliable rules that make our world a more comfortable place to live in. Even in revolutions we don't send all that furniture to the dump. There are too many useful things like wheels and words and bills of rights that we don't want to have to invent all over again.

It does not follow, of course, that everything we keep from the past is useful or good. We are not that smart. Sometimes we hang on to things that we should have sent to the junk pile long ago. We finally threw out slavery in 1863, and no one has suggested that it be revived. But we still hang on to unfair ways of thinking and unfair ways of treating people, ways that began in slavery. When we first adopted the Bill of Rights in the 1790's we did not let slaves have the rights that it is supposed to protect. When the slaves were freed in 1863, they were supposed to get all those rights. But their great-grandchildren are only beginning to get them now. It has taken a hundred years of argument, work, and suffering for the Bill of Rights to get the better of the prejudices inherited from the time of slavery.

It is not just good ideas, then, that are hard to kill but bad ones too. For better or for worse the past stays with us. We change, but we change slowly, and perhaps most slowly of all in our ways of living together.

Who Needs History?

ALL THE WHILE I have been describing the way things and
ideas survive from the past and the way they change and
don't change, I have been hearing in the back of my head an
impatient voice saying, "All right, but how are you going to
end it? Before you get through people will expect you to tell
them that they ought to know about the past in order to
make things better in the future, and you know you don't
want to say that."

And it is true that I don't. Historians and teachers are
always thinking up high-sounding reasons why we (or you!)
ought to study history, how we need to know the past, on the
one hand, in order to avoid repeating its mistakes, or on the
other hand, in order to appreciate and preserve the good
things our ancestors have left us. There may be something
in what they say. We do need to be reminded that we owe
many of the good things in life to the fact that men who lived
and died long ago fought for them. Otherwise we might let

them go and then have to fight for them all over again. That may be why we *ought* to study history; but I think the main reason why people *do* study history is curiosity.

Curiosity is really the main reason why anybody studies anything. You sometimes think of scientists studying atoms in order to make atomic bombs or studying human cells in order to find a cure for cancer. But in fact they study atoms because they want to find out what atoms are; and they study human cells because they want to find out what cells are. If you have ever taken the cover off a watch to see what was inside, you were doing the same sort of thing. You were trying to find out what a watch is. All the microscopes and telescopes and other instruments that scientists use are simply ways of taking the covers off things so you can look inside and see what they are.

Historians study history for the same reason. The past is all around us, making the world the way it is, and historians want to take the cover off, to see what the past is. It is not a very high-sounding reason, but it is a powerful one. And perhaps we can push it a step farther. Is there anything special about the past that makes people feel particularly curious to find out about it?

I have often asked myself this question, and I am not sure about the answer. But I think one reason is that many people, maybe most people, are particularly curious about themselves. We want to know what we are and who we are. There are many ways of trying to get the answer: physiology, psychology, anthropology, and sociology. But history is one of the most important ways. Since so much of what we are comes from the past, we cannot know what we are or who we are without knowing what we have been. When the historian puts together clues to find out about people in the past, he is learning not just about ancient Greeks or Romans or early Americans but about himself and about you and me.

I mentioned earlier that history is mainly about groups, and especially about the large and powerful groups that we call nations. The reason historians have been so curious about groups, I think, is that people learn who they are mainly by finding out about the groups they belong to. If someone meets you on the street of your home town and asks who you are, you probably answer with your own name and the name of your family. You are John Jones or Dorothy Smith. If you did not know what family you belonged to, you would have a hard time saying who you were.

But you are also a Catholic or a Baptist or a Hindu, a New Englander or a Californian, and you are an American. If someone asked you the same question, who are you, when you were walking down the streets of London or Paris, you might tell him not only your name but also that you were an American. In London you would have a hard time explaining who you were if you did not know you were an American. People study the history of the groups they belong to in order to find out what the group is and what belonging to it means. When I say to an Englishman or Frenchman, "I am an American," or even when I just say it to myself, I want to know what it means, and one way to find out is to take the cover off the past and see what Americans have been.

The history of the different nations is not the only thing

that historians study and write about. They study the history of ideas, of science, of religion; they study economic history, social history, the history of anything that has aroused their curiosity. But the kind of history you are most likely to study in school is the history of your own country, the United States. Perhaps you will also study the history of the particular state you live in. And you may also study "world history," which is a pretty big order.

Whatever history you study, there is one last thing to remember: historians are not always right. It is not easy to find out what happened in the past, and sometimes it is very hard to be fair when describing a quarrel, especially a quarrel between your own country and another country. We study history to find out who we are, but sometimes who we are affects the way we read or write history. We are proud of being Americans or Californians or New Englanders or whatever, and we like to see Americans or Californians or New Englanders doing things we can be proud of. We want them to be right, and we are all too likely to think they *were* right just because they belong to the same group that we do.

The only cure for this difficulty is more curiosity. You want to know what really happened, who you really are, not what some historian wishes you were. If the history books you read don't satisfy you, you will have to start taking the covers off things for yourself, looking at the records of the past, putting the pieces together again to see if they really fit. It takes a long time, and by the time you have finished, you may find out one more thing about yourself. You may find that you have become a historian.

Jonathan Strong